Azulejo

In 1492 Abu Abdallah (known in S[
Moorish king of Spain, surrendered
with a cry of desolation, *'el último s*

In the small hot dark Mr Abu Abdallah
lies down on the glazed tiles
his robes folded in a neat pile beside him
his arms gravely holding the shape
of the woman who gravely holds him
as his eyes fill with the night
and he marvels at how there's a word
for every phenomenon in this life
azimuth meaning angle or bearings
algebra meaning reunion of broken parts
algorithm meaning the art of preparing jallab
alcove meaning domed vault
attar meaning perfume – and yet no word
for the way the stuccoed arches
are yawning over him and the scent
of burning catches the back of his throat
how the bones in his buttocks bruise
the thin *mattress* spread out for him
meaning something thrown to the ground
and his eyes can see nothing but night
not *azure* meaning sky-blue nor *zenith*
meaning the sun at its peak
and his mind wanders back to a lost land
the treasure they jettisoned in fleeing
average meaning the proportionate sharing
of storm-damaged goods the basket of *limes*
meaning lemons the chess-board
set out with its king uncastled *rukhkh*
meaning chariot or breath of the phoenix
the queen's black tears streaking her face
kohl meaning the night in her eyes
or the *zero* meaning cipher meaning nought
like the subtle body's sigh as it goes.

Magellan

*Quem sabe se a bordo não seguiria um cistre para acompanhar,
nas noites de calmaria, toadas de marinheiros*˙
— Cristina Drios, 'Mar Magalhães'

For a day and an evening
   we were gathered in an old palace

on the outskirts of the city whose language
   I could read but could not speak.

Beyond the windows the garden floated
   adrift in a squall of low cloud;

the state-room's walls had long since let go
   their decorative papers and delicate frescos,

those electric blues, sea-greens and coral reds
   submitting little by little

to unnumbered summers and winters,
   the bare plaster underneath crazing

finer and finer with every passing century
   of stern atlantic weathers

until it had been transfigured
   into a cartography, endlessly

intricate, of some *terra* forever *incognita*.
   Voices echoed in the vast hall,

cascading down the bow-wave
   of the imperial staircase:

I heard them only as cries
   of sea-birds or a flight of songs

inside the stone. Sometimes the tide
sounds like a foreign tongue,

escutastes as histórias e as canções
sob os céus estrelados de todos os oceanos[†]

– though tonight, becalmed in mid-voyage,
Fernão de Magalhães peers out

over a body of water glassy and taciturn as rock.
Daylight will be a slur of dazzle and haze,

his heart all *saudade*.
In the palace a woman began playing for us,

candlelight caught the silver fan
adorning the guitar's neck,

and what I heard was the lament of water
being poured out on dry ground,

the salt-laden gravity of desire.
Fernão, becalmed in his cabin, dreams

that when if ever he sets sail again
he will reach not land and home but the edge

lying in wait at the far west of the mind,
the sickening sooner-or-later tilt and lurch

on the brink of sleep
for which there is no goodnight prayer

in his or ours or any language,
that his maps and charts are ink on water,

that the future is an immensity
of heave and drop, as intimate

and terrifying as the distance between
　　us and the star-clouds that will ship his name.

The music does what music can:
　　this hairline of gold

running through, then into, the dark.

* Translation: Who knows if, on calm nights, a cittern did not follow them
　on board to accompany the sailors' ditties

† Translation: you have listened to the stories and the songs /
　beneath the starry skies of all the oceans.

Say Goodbye, Catullus

after 'Say Goodbye, Catullus, to the Shores of Asia Minor',
Cy Twombly, 1972–1994, oil, acrylic, oil stick, crayon on three canvases

We moderns are made of lost cities: Athens, Troy, Rome,
their graffiti and generals, their masks and hallucinogens;
or else Verona, Tomis, Alexandria, whose bisexual poets

and citizens-of-nowhere we are, stirring immensities of disquiet;
we are the teeming *civitas*, labyrinthine and violent,
leaking epithalamia and civil war beneath the wheatfields –

and now it's spring again, big skies, his sun-warmed flesh
under your hand, the raw memory of it, and the land convulsing
in gouts of song, uprushes of longing. Time to move on,

you say, but sorrow too has been over-wintering
like some life-form hungry for heat and rut; and now
the jism of grief erupts in a bud-burst of jilt and mucus –

these little chthonic gods are your fellow-travellers,
Gaius Valerius, though you're barely tethered to the earth –
and suddenly your knees buckle with the ache of it,

a barbaric anguish that could blow your brains out –
pain is not an epistemic problem, it's a *cri de sang*,
blood in the yolk, and you – we – a lifetime away from home.

What Is Not Lost

Just sometimes, not everything is lost;
possibilities persist through burn-out

and roof-fall, the ash-heap of oak rafters
and puddles of grey water where panes

of ruby and sapphire, awe and magnificence swim
in the shadows. Transported to childhood,

exhilarated, exhausted, we greet ourselves
and each other as matter, clotted and weeping,

as marks half-buried in a scrawl of vast allusions,
trying our best (which is never enough)

to inhabit the space that has suddenly emptied.
Call it mystery, call it a lacework of stone,

call it a lost cause. Call it a rose.
We are its elements, the light is Kyrie, all-mercy,

call it blaze or the cloudburst that puts out the blaze,
this is not yet an answer to which the question

is hope, that brief blossom of flesh on bare bones
before the sky caves in, the hum of bees like a furnace.

Two Rivers Press has been publishing in and about Reading
since 1994. Founded by the artist Peter Hay (1951–2003),
the press continues to delight readers, local and further afield,
with its varied list of individually designed,
thought-provoking books.

This Thing of Blood & Love

Lesley Saunders is the author of several poetry collections, most recently *Nominy-Dominy* (Two Rivers Press, 2018) and, with Philip Gross, *A Part of the Main* (Mulfran Press, 2018). Her English translations – including the poem that won the 2016 Stephen Spender award – of renowned Portuguese poet Maria Teresa Horta were published as *Point of Honour* (also Two Rivers Press, 2019). Lesley works on collaborative projects with visual artists, sculptors, musicians, photographers and dancers as well as other poets. Otherwise, she is a visiting professor at UCL Institute of Education, London, and an honorary research fellow at Oxford University Department of Education.

Also by Two Rivers Poets

David Attwooll, *The Sound Ladder* (2015)

William Bedford, *The Dancers of Colbek* (2020)

Kate Behrens, *Man with Bombe Alaska* (2016)

Kate Behrens, *Penumbra* (2019)

Adrian Blamires & Peter Robinson (eds.), *The Arts of Peace* (2014)

Charles Baudelaire, *Paris Scenes* translated by Ian Brinton

Conor Carville, *English Martyrs* (2019)

David Cooke, *A Murmuration* (2015)

David Cooke, *Sicilian Elephants* (2021)

Terry Cree, *Fruit* (2014)

Claire Dyer, *Eleven Rooms* (2013)

Claire Dyer, *Interference Effects* (2016)

Claire Dyer, *Yield* (2021)

John Froy, *Sandpaper & Seahorses* (2018)

James Harpur, *The Examined Life* (2021)

A. F. Harrold, *The Point of Inconvenience* (2013)

Maria Teresa Horta, *Point of Honour* translated by Lesley Saunders (2019)

Ian House, *Nothing's Lost* (2014)

Ian House, *Just a Moment* (2020)

Gill Learner, *Chill Factor* (2016)

Gill Learner, *Change* (2021)

Sue Leigh, *Chosen Hill* (2018)

Sue Leigh, *Her Orchards* (2021)

Becci Louise, *Octopus Medicine* (2017)

Mairi MacInnes, *Amazing Memories of Childhood, etc.* (2016)

Steven Matthews, *On Magnetism* (2017)

Henri Michaux, *Storms under the Skin* translated by Jane Draycott (2017)

René Noyau, *Earth on Fire and other Poems* translated by Gérard Noyau
    with Peter Pegnall

James Peake, *Reaction Time of Glass* (2019)

John Pilling & Peter Robinson (eds.), *The Rilke of Ruth Speirs:
    New Poems, Duino Elegies, Sonnets to Orpheus & Others* (2015)

Peter Robinson, *Foreigners, Drunks and Babies: Eleven Stories* (2013)

Peter Robinson, *The Constitutionals: A Fiction* (2019)

Peter Robinson & David Inshaw, *Bonjour Mr Inshaw* (2020)

Lesley Saunders, *Cloud Camera* (2012)

Lesley Saunders, *Nominy-Dominy* (2018)

Jack Thacker, *Handling* (2018)

Susan Utting, *Half the Human Race* (2017)

Jean Watkins, *Scrimshaw* (2013)

Jean Watkins, *Precarious Lives* (2018)

This Thing of Blood & Love

Lesley Saunders

TWO
RIVERS
PRESS

First published in the UK in 2022 by Two Rivers Press
7 Denmark Road, Reading RG1 5PA.
www.tworiverspress.com

ISBN 978-1-909747-96-8

1 2 3 4 5 6 7 8 9

Two Rivers Press is represented in the UK by Inpress Ltd
and distributed by Ingram Publisher Services UK.

Cover image: 'Remembered Present' (2008) © Tom Cartmill

Cover design by Sally Castle
Text design by Nadja Guggi and typeset in Janson and Parisine

Printed and bound in Great Britain by Severn, Gloucester

Acknowledgements

As ever, I am deeply grateful for the supportive efforts of all the people at Two Rivers Press, especially its poetry editor Professor Peter Robinson for the confidence he has shown in my poetry over many years.

Warm thanks are also due to the editors of the following publications in which some of these poems had their first appearance: *Ambit, Analog Sea Review*, Artlyst *Art to Poetry* anthology, Bradford on Avon Arts Festival 2017 website, *Envoi, Ginkgo Prize anthology 2020, Hippocrates Anthologies 2013, 2017* and *2019, Kent & Sussex Poetry Competition Folio* 2020, *New Poetries VI* (Carcanet), Plough Prize 2017 website, *PN Review, Poetry News, Scintilla*, SciPo websites 2018 and 2020, *Ten Poems About Clouds, The Interpreter's House, The SHOp*, TORCH (The Oxford Research Centre in the Humanities) website.

I should like to acknowledge my indebtedness for the name of the book (and of the title poem) to something the critic Jonathan Jones wrote in his article 'Cy Twombly review – blood-soaked coronation for a misunderstood master', *The Guardian*, 30 November 2016.

In 'Fear of Pronouns', the words in italics are a rearrangement of Wikipedia's list of examples of pronouns.

In 'Biopic', the questions are taken from Revlon's advertisement for the company's 1952 lipstick, 'Fire & Ice'.

'Ice Maiden' is based on a case report described by Atul Gawande in *The Checklist Manifesto* (Metropolitan Books 2009).

In 'Minotaur', *'canto hondo'* is, according to the poet Federico Garcia Lorca, a form of primitive song, the oldest in Europe.

The lithograph described in 'Body Art' can be seen on the Wellcome Collection website; the glass fish described in 'Tilapia Nilotica' on the British Museum website; Candace Bahouth's work on her website; some of Louise Bourgeois' textiles on the Tate website; Tom Cartmill's drawings on his website; some of Paula Rego's paintings on the Casa das Historias website; many of Cy Twombly's paintings in various places online; ditto Remedios Varo; some of Joseph Wright's paintings on the Derby Museums website.

Contents

III. Personages

For my beloved family,

whose love makes all things possible

Was there no gentle breeze to warn you?
—Winston Graham, *Marnie*

The voice of the poem – regardless of its gentleness –
necessarily assaults the listener with violence
—David Appelbaum, *Voice*

I. Carnal Knowledge

Croquembouche

A mountain of free-standing choux pastry stuffed
with cream, held together by chocolate and caramel,
then bejewelled with sugared almonds and crystallised
roses, and dusted with icing sugar...

It was Michel Roux holding his frail artifice aloft
in a Paris street *en route* from the *maître-pâtissier*
to his home for a family party that had me
dissolved in tears of disbelief and joy, enfolded
in contemplation of the divine in material form –
such gravity-defying confection, such rich food
for the eyes of the soul, and so preposterously
more than enough to remind us that one day
we too will be as uplifted in rapture as a sugar-rose,
spun finer than a thread of shining caramel,
our sweet flesh will be as candied apricots,
exquisite riposte to catastrophe and apocalypse
and the great night that lies at our feet; incarnated
with all compassion, then broken and consumed.

Carnal Knowledge

Hodie in terra canunt angeli

On this day, another birth. The veil of flesh
you wrap around yourself each time you wake
is a secret you could almost keep – only
your nakedness against hers, the new-mown scent
of you, gives you away, the clear cold undocile
firmament of the elsewhere you've woken from.
In time, you'll perform the ordinary pathology
of bodily being: its corpus of dystrophies, palsies,
nauseas, its *oeuvre* of lesions, cataracts, plaques.
On this day of glories you'll tangle your fingers
in the nest of her hair, touch the tip of her tongue
with yours, still pink as a kitten's – but her soft hide
is a lonely membrane that parts lover from lover,
mother from child, and the only pain relief is the tune
she hums in your ear, her *miserere mei*, as she calls you
her monster, her dayspring, her unforgivable bliss.

Showing Not Telling

Out there on Wide-Awake Hill the white-faced owl
is asking to be lip-read as psyche, as cipher or semaphore,
      a child's name in the ark of a mother's mouth.

Out there in the freezing fog every edge is blunted,
every shape is a grey ghost cast by the meagre search-beam
      of the hunter's mind on the haunted light.

In here where the blizzard is thickest, the house wears
a caul of frost-fur and all the spent chandeliers are ice-harps,
      we play our own version of lost in the dark.

But someplace where the storm has washed us, a radio
fills the sky with verilys and ding-dongs: the self's high holydays
      are numberless. I knew you were you all along.

News

The man has refolded his lightly-smeared napkin
and laid it amid the neat wreck of his breakfast,
he is patting his jacket to make sure his comb
is tucked in the inside pocket behind his wallet.
The clouds are an afterthought, except those
in the tall unflinching panes facing west

whose left-handed light keeps signing itself
on the knuckles of the woman we can't see
clutching a letter. Her convalescent son,
also out of sight, is scanning her face but he can't
read her. There is fever in the American colonies
blossoming beyond the bend in the road

where the freshly-swept lane runs away from itself.
The only sounds now are the tapping
of his cane, champing at every other step,
and the quiet clapping from the attic window.
Nothing is known about Wilma, Matilda,
whatever her name is, on the brink

of crossing the street, she's from another scene
altogether, the sheet of paper she's trying
not to hold on to could rewrite someone's life.
But of course he can't see her
and it's in a language he doesn't understand.
I miss you. We sail for home today.

Biopic

As the Regal's doors close we're buried alive
down velvet aisles. The psyche sees better
in the dark, its heartbreak self swathed
in aliases, wimpled in silvery-noir. Women
die so easily, the slightest cut, a heap
of backless satin, a strapless shoe at the foot
of the stair, the Virginia Slim with Fire & Ice
on its filter, an inch of cooling ash. Have *you*
ever danced with your shoes off? Does gypsy
music make you sad? In a single movement
the audience dons its 3-D lenses and lifts
its gaze to the screen: the nocturnal mammal
looks back through humungous eyes as if
to haunt the men who go on hunting her,
displays the breasts they take as a question
best answered by touching, tell each other
she's flirting with fire, skating on ice.
Her fingertips match her lips, but she won't
be healed by birdsong, its inglorious roses.
Do you secretly hope the next man you meet
will be a psychiatrist? Me too. Me too.

You Bring Out the Bourgeois in Me

I am still a girl trying to understand myself
— Louise Bourgeois

Please don't wake me. Walking on my hands
through dream-suburbs of green belt, the gabled

house-fronts of Ickenham, I must slumber on
through volumes of obsession-diaries, feeding

myself with my clever girl's fingers, tongue grown
too big for my mouth. Lying in my stockinette

of lard, stitched pig-of-me, I feel for dints or lumps
in this pillow of body; with my glass look like a doll's

I monitor the leak of puberty, the filthy pink
of fat and brassière. I am your belovèd daughter,

bandaged and snoring, sewn up in my name-tapes.
Bleed.   Eat.   Sleep.   Cry.   Cogitate.   Chew my food

into mothers-and-fathers as the quarrelling starts.
What I want is a wand of light, my thoughts rising

like dew-smoke off the roof-felt, the brakes and creeks
of all the Americas to come swimming in my eyes.

Fear of Pronouns

I love you. That reminds me
of something. Take it
or leave it. Anyone can
do that. Who would say
such a thing?

Myself, I've a morbid fear
of crinolines and sword-play,
the weaponised grammar,
the whole yin-yang he-she
hoo-ha of too much information,

our little fantasies of authority
and desire. He's shell-shocked,
she's hysterical, I'm phobic:
it reminds me of the wide open
spaces I'm afraid to cross,

the continent of empty streets,
the plate glass floor nine storeys up.
I've filled my rooms with furniture,
my shelves with sexless china bowls
of blueish green. Pain makes one

inventive; I've put them there
to trap the neutralities of dust
and daylight. Tomorrow I'll be
on a train, the I-est mode
of travel, while watching a skater

roll out the miles between us
in a glory of epicene motion.
Who would say such a thing? Anyone
can do that. Take it or leave it. That
reminds me of something. I love you.

Devices & Desires

How does the water of the brain turn into the wine of consciousness?
— David Chalmers, *The Conscious Mind: In Search of a Fundamental Theory*, 1997

If you gotta ask, you ain't never gonna get to know
— Galen Strawson, *Realistic Monism: Why Physicalism Entails Panpsychism*, 2006

My small fingers used to prise my father's eyelid open as it drowsed – peering closely at the globe glistening whitely in its tegument of flesh, I'd ask 'You still in there, Daddy?' He invariably answered 'No' – which is how I knew there must be a ghost in the machine, an insubstantial man in the moon who sat inside my father's head and dreamed his dreams for him while he slept. I liked to imagine all the quiet whirring, like the cuckoo in our clock or the silver swan I watched in a castle once, swimming gracefully through the river's glass while music played, and bending low to chase a little fish.

I often marvel at how well we've been constructed, as pleasure-seeking, pain-avoiding engines whose springs and bellows, ratchets and keys have been so skilfully gloved in skin, padded with flesh-tinted silks and leathers, and are redolent with the mysterious musks of qualia. Here we come, jerking our own strings, tippy-toed and double-jointed, jaws clacking and feet clattering on the wooden stage. Ach, I'm talking to myself again: Descartes' fault, no doubt – I'm just sad I'll never know what it's like for a bat to be a bat.

Placebo

If you think about it, a kiss on the cheek when you fall over
is a placebo
— Dr Clare Gerada, chairwoman of the Royal College
    of General Practitioners

Am I so hard to please? It's said red pills
work less efficiently than blue or yellow ones
(though Latin can be a panacea in itself),
the side-effects of self-deception hidden
in the small print on the maker's leaflet
folded into a wad inside the packet –
better to self-medicate with a boxed set
of afternoon crime dramas where shoulders
are prosthetised with satin pads and blood's
shed recklessly as claret on Turkish rugs:
libations to the jealous watchful gods,
the things done and left undone that upbraid me
in the night, their abrasions and wistful pains
as of a missing limb. In the grey hour of morning
or was it far into evening a glimmer of insight
pale as aspirin hovered in the pathless orchard
of my mind like a salvific, and finally I realised
there's no pleasing to be had, no clemency
for *tristitia*. I sit here in my elegant skin, implacable.

Wishful Thinking

The modern science of happiness enables us to measure people's
quality of life in meaningful ways
— Centre for Economic Performance, London School of Economics

Happiness is a science. We make our own luck,
a glimpse of plane trees through the narrow gully
between here and now, a spill of old-fashioned roses
in the still of a shadowless evening, the happy hour
of blackbird-song *im wunderschönen Monat Mai.*
All this laughter will lead to tears – though these too
can be measured: a thimble, a river, an ocean,
a clown's. Like anyone else I want to be told
about randomised control trials, the soul-searching
and ethical dilemmas of double-blinding,
the treatment of scurvy by oranges and lemons
compared with a daily quart of cider, or even
the strange case of the lady who could tell you
whether someone had poured the milk or the tea first
in her afternoon cup. Such experiments are inspiring,
numbers touch us with their therapeutic power
like happy pills, the null hypothesis presumes us
innocent. But lovers know what wickedness is,
the haplessness of being human, the wilderness of life.
They are coins in the fountain, a leap in the dark,
they have not given their consent, they do not hope for cure.

Love Heart

after 'Box of Delights', Candace Bahouth, installation

When the taxi came and her parents departed in their astrakhan coats and a haze of aftershave and *Nuits de Paris*, she'd climb the stairs to their bedroom and pull open the great cedar-wood door of their wardrobe. She'd slide her feet into the teeter-heeled slippers, nestle her face in taffeta stoles and silk kimonos, drape her mousy hair with loops of diamante and marcasite, lift the swansdown powder puff out of its box and dab it over her cheeks, take sips of air out of one of the dainty gold-rimmed cups that lay on the cut-glass tray, leave a *moue* of scarlet on the fragile porcelain.

It was like Love Hearts melting on her tongue.

But never enough, it was never enough.

One day shortly after her thirteenth birthday the willow-pattern dinner plate slipped and broke like the sky before rain. She wept into her hanky. She stooped and swept and gathered, all the petals and smithereens, the feathers and seashells, the spilled sequins and alabaster ballerinas, the scattered baubles and china roses, the tiny saltspoons and shattered mirrors, the rose-red and snow-white, the fly-away blue and spun-sugar gold. Glued them together in a tower of many-spouted teapots as tall as a house: a samovar of elixirs, totem to the gods of too-much. The bower and the glory, for ever and a day.

Her lips smeared with lollipop and cherryade, she sits tracing the giant peonies on the wallpaper with her finger, looking from time to time out of the window and waiting for her beautiful parents to come home. Bits and pieces of her lie around on the floor, in case anyone, anyone at all, should rush in and crush them underfoot.

Balletomania

The tyranny of 'The Nutcracker' is emblematic of how
dull and risk-averse ballet has become
— Sarah Kaufman, *The Washington Post*

Marie is about to cut herself badly, falling
into the glass cabinet – her other name
is Clara, as if she were see-through. Blood
everywhere. It's almost too late for exegesis;

we've learnt, as her family members sleepwalk
towards her, to recognise such obvious symbols –
though many critics have broken their teeth
on this particular chestnut. It's as clear as day,

plain as the nose, even if no-one believes her:
it's hard to swallow what young women get up to
these days, their bodies suddenly flooding
with desire – it can take weeks for soul-doctors

to invent a cure, for the mice to look like mice
again. She is lethal, airy, weightless; bandaged
from head to foot, ruthlessly vulnerable.
If we threaten to steal her dolls and fairy-cakes

perhaps we can de-radicalise her. But she lolls
in bed pretending to convalesce, her cot facing
the window and its grey sea, the light's cold hand
on her neck. Marzipan men march to her rescue,

the mice nibble the reeking hem of her dress.
In this land of sugar and spice and slave-trade
she'll dance on, seeking solace for her dead daddy.
We fidget with our costumes, waiting our turn.

The Heart of Doctor Coppelius

It was a casket, planed and japanned,

a handcrafted box with a quartet of drawers
that opened and shut in time to a clock
whose knock only he could hear in the dark –

though what greeted them first was the ghost

of a perfume, lingering scent of an arboreal past:
oak, or perhaps rosewood, a bird-loving
durable species with its foot in the earth.

They want to undo it, prise its dovetails apart,

use the blunt edge of a knife to uncouple it,
with their fingers inspect the way it's been fitted
in intricate removable pieces so they can scry

how the nice quirks of its mechanism work.

The remarkable thing is the faint burst of song
as they lay it all out in the light.

Body Art

after 'Partial dissection of the chest of a man'
—Jacob Chr. Roux, lithograph, 1822

He has found a brief peace, you might think,
listening to the lieder music in his head,
its sad tenor line like a vein of grey sky
spilling across an inland sea. The linen stole
they lent him has slipped in a décolleté
from his shoulders, so the whole of his light

can suddenly be seen. A woman might faint
at the way his heart reveals itself so,
how the still life of him will be laid down
on handmade paper, the one love-song
he did not write her. In his long dream
he is scoring his body as an anthem of darkness

while we hide from ourselves under our leathers,
pretending not to know this other who is us.

The Silent Teachers

Anatomy is a vocabulary of selfhood
— Michael Sappol, *Visionary Anatomies*, 2004

They get under your skin, these engravings
and *écorchés*, these intimate pop-up autopsies
in wax and papier-mâché, these dead ringers
of the living, playing with our notions of who
or what we are. Pinned to a wall, the tree of life
has been stripped to its bone, feathery dendrites
ferning into wintry espaliers of pleasure, pain,
aortic wires shrilling with inaudible chords –
here are our stilled lives, abject and fallible,
flayed and splayed on the table, friable, fluid,
liable to leakage, breakage, spoilage. Tear off
the shroud, lift the flap to view Eve's womb;
grab hold of the cold hand, coil your fingers
in the wound, greet the beauty's lidless stare:
this is where art and science meet. Come,
join the dance – the rest is grist and thin air.

Sleuth

Her hands like roots feel under the hood
of turf for tics and fetishes, migraines,
pieces of smashed china the colour of sky
in childhood, scenes that the unwary
may find upsetting. Fire had gutted the site
before the flood came and wept it away,
though symptoms of fallout and trauma
jut like ribs through the grass. Some stories
are best seen from the air, a google of ley lines
and land mines: this is an infant science,
theory at the mercy of practice, fingertip
fieldwork, divination of signs, dream-diaries:
here's a *trou de loup* for the wolf man;
over there a study in shell-shock, a casebook
of opiates and conjectures. You hear a song
yesterday and find yourself singing it today,
emotions most people prefer to keep hidden –
though terrible things are impossible to forget.
She wraps our phantom limbs in bandages,
lays a stethoscope to the ticking bomb.

A Suspicious Science

A career in forensic entomology may not be for the faint of heart
— Crime Scene InvestigatorEDU.org

Sung Tz'u knew what every insect needs:
fast food, a place to breed, a warm house
to call its own. Smelling the volatile molecules
of death from thirty *li* away, a cloud of flies
had settled on the guilty sickle. Case closed,
in a paddy field nearly nine centuries ago.
Elsewhere and today, bluebottles hatch
from eggs to maggots in a single balmy day,
hister beetles arrive to gorge on the larvae,
followed by mite-hordes and chewing moths.
Corpse-reading is the washing away of wrongs,
water will be ladled through the fontanelle
to decipher by what route this death arrived.
In the mountains the climate is constant,
plums must be salted and dried for a poultice,
there are three hundred and sixty-five bones
in a man's skeleton, one for each night of the year.
Do not be deterred by the smell. Invertebrates
will continue to arrive at their appointed hour:
the hollow chest, the swollen belly of the beast
have become a home. It's where the heart is,
and how you can tell the precise time of decease
wherever the body happens to be found,
life-size and rapt in its reveries under a watery sun.

Prime Suspect

People are nostalgic for an Agatha Christie type of world
— Mathew Prichard, Agatha Christie's grandson

What used to stymie the detective
was the severed telephone line,
the urgent but undelivered telegram
or the possibility of getting lost
down a country lane in the dark –
quaint old-lady plot-lines these days,
stale excuses in the bone-china drama
of afternoons. I was brown and lean
from the garden and clearing out
Mother's house at the end of summer.
There was a suitcase under the bed
in the spare room, cookbooks, ludo,
paperbacks with pencilled exclamations
that exposed a rampant cryptosemia.
Later I went swimming off the coast
of Cornwall, floating there on my back
and staring up into rimless skies. Facts
give nothing away, though there are clues
in the shapes of cloud, the grey tide
of pebbles on the beach, the drift
of dreams. You can end up reading
too much into solitaire, spend undue hours
on your knees hunting the truant piece
of Venetian lagoon. I kept the mirror
with the seashell frame, the madeira glasses
and the scissors she used for cutwork.
I didn't find the dented silver thimble
(also known as a kiss), the chinese whispers
or the cat's cradle. So it's comforting to know
a train can still be missed, a splinter
turn to sepsis, the wrong pills swallowed.
You won't detect a true-life crime in all of this –
it was only ever her word against mine.

Herr B. or Beauty and the Beast: excerpts from case-notes

… At this point, Herr B. became very agitated, making as if to arise and leave; I too sprang to my feet, but forbore from restraining him and so, for a moment, we were each suspended as it were in mid-air.

I persuaded him to sit again. In paraphrase, this is the dream that he went on to recount: 'Much later, the girl re-appears at the street door, alone, without her parents or even her beloved dachshund. Quite bemused and hesitating to invite her in, I – clothed now only in nightshirt and carpet slippers – question her with a look; for her part, also without saying a word, she gives me to understand that this is a matter of the utmost urgency. Beneath her youthful beauty lie a fearful sorrow and longing. I step aside and admit her to my rooms. Something happens next that I cannot recall; although afterwards I feel as if a great burden has been lifted from me.'

I have previously noted that it is my intention to use the forensic arts of modern detection to bring to light long-buried psychic matter and thus to solve the great mysteries of human behaviour. I am, in a manner of speaking, attempting to decipher the fingerprints of the soul. Nonetheless, as I took in his words, I experienced the gravest dilemma of my professional life, and I steeled myself to acknowledge that I was hearing the confession of a crime of the most depraved and bestial nature.

Then Herr B. emitted a hoarse sob from behind his hands, which he held clenched like paws over his face. After a while he continued with his story, haltingly and with many false starts and long pauses, until evening was upon us and I stood up to light the lamps. As I continued to listen to Herr B.'s account, I found myself unable (or perhaps unwilling) to decide with any finality of judgement whether his was a case of intractable self-delusion or of authentic redemption.

In the flickering shadows, the wretched man appeared more animal than human, unshaven and hunched, full of self-pity and shame, yet also strangely suffused with an innocence, a kind of grace. We sat for an hour in silence. And then I remembered my own dictum, to wit, that after every other explanation has been eliminated, what remains, however improbable, must be the truth.

Demos

Man has within him a divine thing, the intellect
— Aristotle, *Nicomachean Ethics*

My dream told me this, that the weals on the flesh of my neck needed to be seen under Greek light, so I clambered through an impossibly narrow aperture to stand in its search-beam. It turned out I was in the grip of another flare-up of auto-inflammatory illness, a migraine of *idées fixes*, bone-stiffening anxiety, an eczema of chronic irritability, even a brief outbreak of mouth-ulcerating hate-speech. There are no anti-allergens for the biochemistry of anger and politics, for the ghosts in the self's machine that act like foreign bodies breeding visitations and voices; only untreatable dreams, luciferous and virulent, of havoc, of a land flayed and suppurating, of the *polis* plagued by a pandemic of lies. I got out of bed and dressed, every cell of my being a miniature engine of toxic waste, the thrilling taste of adrenalin in my mouth.

Block

Nothing to cry about, I told myself, although I

could never seem to sit still despite my windows'
slow gold, my garden deep with hedged light
blowing its violet theology out into the dusk.

There was a thought at the edge of my eye,
a dog-star in the dark of my mind that I ought not
to look at, even sideways or with my eye-mask on.

I have done nothing wrong, I think, only the usual,
the obvious, *nobis quoque peccatoribus*, no actual
violence, no knives or guns; just a smidgen of bad faith.

I switch channels, refresh the screen. Nothing doing.
In one of the soaps a woman's sobbing rescues me,
like a sudden soakaway appearing in the road

or something covered with a blanket in the wood.

All That Summer

All summer long I was under the microscope,
on my way to becoming a someone, the whiff
of old books and Windolene on my fingers.
I regretted nothing except what I would fail at,

alfresco sex in all-out Hebridean rain for example,
living blithe-mindedly, or articulating the empathy
I genuinely felt. I noticed the insomniac weather
was breeding storm flies, they were feeding

on my little compositions of avocado rinds, stinking
gladioli, withered persimmons. My conversations
tied themselves in knots till I was truly longing
for parthenogenesis; I kept checking my age-spots

in my grandmother's compact, couldn't get enough
of the Tudors, their televisual sense of fragile
alliances. Today should have been a Campari-and-soda
moment, but the anguish of it, this only life, demands

I magnify myself beyond what is possible, display
impossible generosity: I shall not be able now
like a child's jewelled glove to have my dreams soothed
out of me. The scent of rotting fruit. Then thunder.

Vacation

Dog days. The whole place drugged with heat,
    all the books stolen from bedrooms,

men moving in to deal with the drains.
    It is getting harder to sleep, no shelter

even in the hallucinogen of dreams
    from the lack of breeze or anything like

surprise. Conference delegates get
    through breakfast decently enough,

inquiring after bus times, the quickest way
    to the botanic garden, the most typical pub

with Irish music. We pass from ritual
    to theology on a knife-edge, anxious

to placate the grain-gods, keep them
    attentive, however impractical it seems

in this bleached economic climate.
    They must on no account be eaten.

Afternoon lasts forever, under its dustcovers
    all furniture is ghost. Out in the wide world

small apples redden as if by metempsychosis.
    Let it all return now, the winter coats, the voices.

II. Vital Signs

On Not Knowing

The nature of regret is delicate, a door
that should have been there, but is not;

what happened back up in the hills
was a matter of luck, nothing personal –

the fact of the forests, the leaf-moths,
the fork in the road. (There are no images,

save for the river running to sand, salt
on the tongue, the pulse of previous stars.)

Mean Time

On Saturday evening three of my clocks were playing tricks:
the LCD on the kitchen windowsill clicked backwards
as I watched; the bedroom radio alarm was running
twenty minutes slow; and on my mother's marbled timepiece

the smallest hand slewed and stumbled, ticked itself
continually back to six. On the way home I'd seen the spew
of feathers in the road like the innards of a blattered pillow,
half the grey sky spilt and draggled on the ground, a day

split through the middle, rare as a cuckoo – some airy thing
brought down, unmade, displayed in all its solemn gadgetry.
Tonight the nation's clocks rewind, take pity on the quick, the dead.

Collapse

This is what makes me cry, I thought,
and the light was blowing sleeve-like
through self-Novembering aspens as my door
flew open to let in a swarm of leaves

and the wasps went on falling out of the air,
the dark hasps of their wing-cases gaping
and shutting in brassy whispers till the carpet
was writhing with yellow beelzebubs

and the young queens whirled like dervishes
as the new weather stabbed in from the pole,
leaving a grain of agony-gold on their lips.

This is what makes me cry, I said, and the thought
that something north-like had turned in its sleep,
was wreaking its truth under my eaves.

Vital Signs

There are no means of reversing the process which is melting
the polar ice caps
— Mayer Hillman, environmental researcher and campaigner

Some days I've crept upstairs
and lain down on the foldaway bed –
the arid air and locked drawers,
the cracked cloudless wallpaper
in this domain of late afternoon
are the dormitory of dark dreams,
the corners where I've left hopes
to forget them; the bowed shelves
hold thesauri of old words like reedbed,
mudflat, shingle, fen. Safe as houses.
My springtime consolable selves
hang like fur-moths from the rails
and the snail that scaled the curtain
last September has become a small
round hole in the sky of the ceiling.
Moments later, I find myself taking
a shortcut, driving the car into water,
a flood that came out of nowhere
and swallowed the summer road.
This is not my house after all.

For Other Bees Do Not Visit This Flower

I have very little doubt that if the whole genus of humble-bees
became extinct in England, the heartsease and red clover would
wholly disappear
— Charles Darwin, *On the Origin of Species*, 1866

Some hearts fracture slowly, a small crack
in the muscle wall deepening over the years,

and the sound of breathing more like sobbing,
as though floodwaters were swamping the airways –

the storms are getting oftener and stronger,
their muster of names those of long-lost cousins

blowing home from overseas, bringing gifts
of biblical proportions and rattling with stories;

we hunch inside our skins, trying not to listen.
But old houses are porous, on a winter's evening

you can smell the smoke of other people's fires
through the depleted walls, like bad news drifting in,

a waft of paranoia. Then something we should not
have said flies out of our mouths, a dead word

like bumblebee or heart's-ease. In the small hours
in flowerless chambers the planet trembles.

Clouded Silver

A moth, not so much a self-portrait
as a slight erasure of light;
not so much a moth as a mother
– one who catches her breath
like a window about to fly open.
So many earrings, it's nearly a theory
of everything, right at her fingertips.
The art-deco wardrobe is monstrous,
crammed with nostalgic frocks
and foxes with jet beads for eyes,
a looking-glass blossoming with clouds.
The gale inside is a kind of goodbye
to the purely personal, the ars poetica
turning into a power struggle
between Paris and New York, opals
and diamonds, the bareback rider
and the tightrope walker, mother
and child. She is not me
though the eyebrows are similar,
one permanently raised in query.
What do you do with that kind of grief?

The Coming

In time the wind will come and destroy my lemons
— Cy Twombly

I would like to be able to paint you
the weight of cornfields *ante bellum*,

their walls of elegant sky scrawled on
by something that is neither

memory nor prediction; more
a small shudder down the spine

of the dogwood trees, as if the land
could read the wind and how terribly

it can turn, how the whole night
could become white with meltwater,

how fruit-pickers might gather at the far edge
and watch their tents filling like sails.

Some Trees

Here are some trees whose wood burns sweetly:
sandalwood, rosewood, eucalyptus, juniper, cedar.

And these are trees whose resin is sweet when burnt:
camphor, frankincense, hashish, myrrh. Their smoke rises

like prayer; their scent is invisible, untouchable,
like god. Believers say god is present in the smoke.

Incense is the sweat of trees – when burnt, its fumes
create mind-altering volatile hydrocarbons which migrate

to the olfactory nerve and the amygdala, enhancing
receptiveness to the sacred, bringing god down to earth.

The trees burn and prayers are prayed in the presence
of the smoke, whose smell, untouchable, is everywhere,

like god. Here are some creatures who are learning
smoke: koala, dunnart, echidna, goanna, bandicoot, cockatoo.

And this is a magpie who has learnt a new call: it rises
like prayer through the smoke, mimicking the sound

of the sirens of the ambulances and fire-engines.
Here are some trees whose wood is burning, not sweetly.

Berg

She's a Jungfrau, a Brunhild,
she thinks there is only ice – icicle,
diamond-dust, rink, her whole world
is an Hôtel de Glace, a shadowless castle
utterly glitter and glass, filigree and brittle,
ice birds twinkling in ice trees.
Ice wants everything exquisite,
to freeze it with a kiss, call it
Tuktoyaktuk, Semersuaq;
has blanked how it feels to run, be river,
drinkable, salty, quag.
She's titanic.

Oh but hear her chirrup and groan,
the iron-clad throat-singing,
her jingling wind-chimes floating over
the vitrified fields of Marylebone, Piccadilly,
as the ice-breaker westerlies petition her,
testing the quizzical hollows
of her anklebones, nudging and nuzzling
the spectral backs of her knees,
feathering her skater's insteps
until the arctic hem of her frock
begins waltzing and she loosens, molten,
catastrophic.

Glaciarium

...it has been surmised that there was a time when
the circumpolar ice extended far into the temperate zone
— Robert Chambers, *Vestiges of the Natural History
of Creation*, 1844

From here as you skate you can look at the Alps,
backdrop to your catch-foot, your spread eagle;
as you jump over your hat you can glimpse
the tree-line of larches above your bare head,
the balustrade of players who scrape out
a polka with chilblained fingers, a fine steam
beading their velveteen cuffs. Behind the walls
and high passes, always half in towering shade,
are other objects your eye cannot follow,
the way being blocked by sundogs or a stranger
who when you wake is your own phantom-self
thrown by the sky across a mountain of cloud.
This is the year the earth has suddenly grown
so much older than anyone had counted on,
its genealogies inscribed in fossiliferous rock,
its archives deep-frozen in glacial spillways
where only frost-flowers bloom. But today
is the day when the ice-maker fails, you lose
your footing as the cosmos tilts and the rink
runs ruinedly into its constituent fluids.
You can't see yet what's coming over the hill,
hurtling towards you from way before Genesis:
an alp-man riding the flood-tide with a gutful
of deer-meat inside him, his skin-leather leaking
unstoppable secrets. In your sleep you're still
skating, endlessly tracing a figure of eight
through the deepest of winters – now or soon
with a small force throw your body forwards into light.

Hazy, Massed, Dappled

Annuaire Météorologique 1802, Jean-Baptiste Lamarck

Hazy, massed, dappled, their cotton shifts, their furs and velvets; bringers of lambs' tails and almond-blossom, suspended ceilings of heartbroken thunder and storm-damaged childhoods – you are never as alone as you think you are. But in the walled garden all that fills you is sky and the wisps of someone else's weathers: spring snow, a rag of fire in a bare tree, roofs smoking with dew-mist. A cirrus of midges. Then sunlight bursting each pane of glass as it passes, like a housemartin crashing softly against the picture-rails. Afternoon darkening in all its parlours and pigeon-holes of grey. Now move hands like clouds (seven times). Carry tiger to mountain.

This Thing of Blood & Love

after 'Study for Achilles Mourning the Death of Patroclus',
Cy Twombly, 1962, ballpoint pen and graphite

This is not a love poem.
Because grief is flood & drought assailing conjointly,
because Achilles is consumed by a firestorm
of desire & rage & longing, because love's relics
cannot smile back at him nor make a feral nest
of the bedclothes, because they cannot howl out in lust
nor sing him to sleep, cannot assuage his headache,
because they cannot delicately and with a long tongue
suck the honeydew from his thigh, because the eyebright
& the hairstreak are just names, because Patroclus
is just a name, because the hare & the nightingale,
the slow-worm & turtle dove, because they insist
on getting themselves killed, because these flowers of love-
sickness, this ghost of something like a rose, are all that's left,
because he scribbles the name again, crosses it out, again,
because the thread or stalk or stem or cord or feeler of it
is as red as life, because it is a thing of love and blood,
because he is blown, deracinated & visceral, towards it
in every fibre of his being, because he is trying to record how
the news smote him, what the ash in his hair smelt of.
Because he needs witnesses. Because he bleeds. Wants to.
Because this is not a love poem, only a study for one.

Carbon Angel

for Lisa Kopper

Not asking for more clarity
than necessary, I could grow old
here, trying to stand my ground
as this stern avatar of carbon
– unmelting, rust-resistant –
robs me of oxygen, wraps me
in ashes, abrades my light
with its diamonds. I dipped
my fingers in my own blood
to war-paint my face one day
when I still bled; the image
in the mirror nearly threw me
from the room, and I saw angels
can be charcoal as well as star.

Now my sight is not so good,
the right eye turns straight lines
into waves, a ripple of energy
running unbidden and river-like
across my optic field: a late style,
unquiet, contrarian. And still
all that has ever lived lives on
in coal or peat or pitch, what flows
like oil will resurrect as firefly-gold,
then burn to a purgative red
and the ten million more colours
the seen world is made of.
There is no time to waste.
This is the angel whose look
cremates flesh, whose breath
is roses and gunpowder,
whose terrestrial name is love,
faithful and vast as forest fire.

III. Personages

The Light of the World

after 'A Philosopher giving that Lecture on the Orrery, in which
a lamp is put in place of the Sun', Joseph Wright of Derby,
oil on canvas, *c.* 1776

Read nothing into this. We are men
of science, not superstition. The light
that shines here is the lamp of knowledge,

the zeal in our eyes is the fire of ideas,
the ardent industry of thought. Our maker
creates his suns and moons with minerals

of earth – cakes of Naples yellow, carmine lake,
a ground of whitish gypsum bound in oil.
And here's his epiphany: a working cosmos,

its meridians, orbits, spheres. The godly things,
the priceless gifts we bring, are those of wonder,
not of worship. Read everything into this.

Bi-polar

after 'Vesuvius in Eruption, with a View over the Islands
in the Bay of Naples'
— Joseph Wright of Derby, oil on canvas, *c.*1776

Yet something can be two things at once:
fire and granite, moon and water, vision
and pigment; oil and soul. Sulphur seas

roil beneath our feet, a cloud's mutability
is glued on jute; merry walks perforce
with melancholy. So I make these perilous

studies of the light the more to know
the quality of dark, its gravity, its allure.
Everything I paint is Nature, all is artifice,

the artist's trance is of the real. Night
and the volcano engineered this earth: man
and monster, we stand across their work.

Malaria

after 'Paludismo', Remedios Varo, gouache and cardboard, 1947

In the eye of his fever, the rush and blind of the storm suddenly stills. Sick with longing he can see nothing but glare, lifting his head, his mind, to stare at the lace the brightness is wearing, its hair: bindweed, millipede ivy, old man's beard, the swell and upwelling of greenwood, *terre verte* in all its true colours summoning him home from his *triste tropique* to a once-known world. But this noise like nightfall is only those gauze-winged traffickers in gold and blood, who seethe under the lid of his brain till his brief air is crammed with incurable light.

Drawn

for Tom Cartmill

With any treatment we're never far from the sea, its attention
to detail, its stargazers and myriad transparent bone-eaters,
the way it calls out in the night – the sound of wet black ink
on paper, suitable for being sung aloud, is the true devotional
nature of the work, chthonic as well as benthic. (*I can't tell you
why it made me so happy, I just know that it did.*) Width, height,
depth; perception, perception, perception, patinated as if
change was always this narrow border of aging and exposure,
or else a carpet of gallant exuberance. Every league of the way,
Sicily, Spain, Aotearoa, the sequences and tessellations, peaks
and troughs, arabesque and pungawerewere, how it all fits
together and falls apart. *Horror vacui*: no serious artist should
ignore this. (*I was full of something, the day could not contain me.*)

A Theory of Turquoise

'Do we yet perceive all the colors there are?'
— Erin Hoffman, *The Wine-Dark Sea: Color and Perception
   in the Ancient World*

Looking west, the eye sees
only glaze and shimmer,
a gloom of ultramarine
the Greeks called wine-dark.
When you live by the sea,
you carve it with beaked prows,
dimple it with nets, blaze and
blister it with pearl-diver's lungs;
your vision adjusts. Sometimes
the only movement you'll make
is to scan the horizon for sails
that loom like war, then
drop your gaze to the shoreline,
its small white bones, antlers
of oak, sea-glass. These
are the colours called *glaukos*,
khloros, grey with wildfire
behind it, or pale as grass
in the noon-haze, aqueous-
vitreous like the hollow orb
of a wave. Turn eastwards,
and the whole scene shifts:
Troy.
Troy with all of Persia at its back,
the tiled oasis-palaces, domes
inlaid with robin's-egg and gold,
oiled beads and studded bridles
like fireflies in the indigo twilight,
jaspers and jades and lapis lazuli,
bezel-rings to ward off unfaithfulness
or sudden death, a thousand bowls

of cloudless ocean simmering
along the barbarian coast –
blue mirrors where we might look
to glimpse something precisely
not ourselves. The Greeks
could find no name for this.

Palinurus

For those who sail, the knowledge of the seas
is the art of gazing at stars – how to see them
by looking slightly away; and then how to open
one's ears to the tales they tell of navigation,
of long homecomings after war and heartbreak.
The stars of your ocean, Palinurus, were sown
into sea-song and memory – of how, driven on by
the self's changeable weathers, you rowed out
into the bay, staring back at the familiar domes
and parasol pines going up in smoke, ghosting.
Breakfast on board was sweet and brief, cheese, figs,
when the storm, towering overhead, threw you
to the deck – a *meltemi* out of the north, out of
nowhere in a glorious turquoise sky. Now
your sense of taste – of salt and wet and ice –
is a new kind of seeing while wave after wave
is blinding you and the breath's being sucked
from your lungs by the three-day gale. The sea
copies itself, twice over, tiny and pitch-dark
in your eyes as you scan the black wall of water –
no moon, only a judder in the air, a fold in the night
where light is in hiding. Yes, in your mind you know
where to find them, Arcturus, Orion, the Bears,
the April rainers, and the stream of celestial fireflies
that spill over your bare arms, milk-white seeds
smelling of distance, Hesperia. But you no longer
belong to yourself, there is still too much
you do not know: why the wave-tug on the shingle
hisses like the *maïstros* gusting in an olive tree,
and what song you will sing as you dive to the bottom
fishing for sea-lilies or the *noctilucae* silvering like stars.

Tilapia Nilotica

A soul swimming towards the afterlife
like a glint of sun eeling through reeds
is NebAmun
NebAmun the official
NebAmun in his papyrus skiff and great bead collar
heading for the lightwells the deadhouse

Hidden in the sleeve of his tunic is a glass fish
he will sometimes touch to remind him
(NebAmun the husband)
of the teeming tilapia pools
the pleasure-gardens of the reed-marsh
the blue lotus-lilies their juice

He will weigh it in his dry palm
this ripple of light with the desert at its core
and in the vial of its striped belly
a mist of sandalwood cassia cardamom
to scent the nostrils of the dead
NebAmun

My Little Eye

How to account for this friendless feeling
when everywhere is surveillance,
an all-you-can eat party held *in camera*

for loners, those who do not wear wives
under their coats to remind them of home?
In a tight corner they travel knightwise

till they're off the board, out of the frame,
leaving the king *solus*, celibate, a self-portrait
of an eye. All voyeurs now, spies stationed

in the walls, we're made to watch the pageantry
exactly as it happens, the tanks moving in,
the cut lines and house arrests, the straight miles

light hurtles along. The hostess plays queen,
takes our bouquet of gazes without a smile.

En Passant

On the pavement is a table, laid for two,
the pieces already in play; a single chair.
You are the invisible opponent seated
behind a drift of curtain, waiting
for someone to pass by, then retrace,
up for the game, curious. A quarter-hour
chimes; another, then the o'clock.
The heat buzzes, the street's drone-and-chatter
skitters round the room; the river
sparkles and stinks of drains.
                                        You move
a pawn, hover it over the empty square
in a gambit so effortlessly elegant
that you tilt your head to the applause
you can almost hear. Soon the castles
will creep their shadows across the board,
the cavalrymen will jingle their spurs,
the queen will rouse herself from her reverie,
touch up her lipstick. But who will rescue
the king from his aloofness, his brilliance?

Glass Man

The war peters out in ruined orchards, faint sounds
of rubble settling in the dead hours, a metallic smoulder
on the edge of towns. Then plague. These are the years
when a man might dream his body is as frail as butter,
lighter than a feather, that his head will roll, that his brain
and bones have turned to glass. He knows he'll shatter
at a touch, he's an exploding teardrop, a flawed solitaire.
Hiding his face in crystalline hands, he falls and falls
through the cloudless houses of his body, half-blinded
by their brittle brilliance. A gift of vision, say physicians,
to scry the soul with such clarity, such self-clairvoyance:
but he only stares at his feet and sees the melting sand
in which he stands, the lime-pits, the flame-throwers.

Dark

In memory of the many miners who continue to lose their lives
in disasters that should not have happened

Say instead there are thirteen types of dark, starting with the soft
dark of a child's or sweetheart's flung-out sleep like spilt milk
across the night, and this they call slumber. Next,

the opulent darks of red, as in danger, shame, salvation,
also the perfunctory dark of a dozen unread dossiers;
then the faltering dark that trails off the edge of a torch beam

like an unfinished sentence, the walker hurrying to rescue
what still might be saved; previously, the dark of a blind eye turning,
the collapse as of a lung and all its carved and vivid airways,

the pitch-black of no other voice at the end of the line,
of the names and evasions that stay in everyone's throats;
later there's the shadow of the shadow of hope, the ash

which is called despair; finally the permanent invisible dark
of daytime in the houses they left with all the lights burning.

Ice Maiden

How else were we to save her?

Cold has so many ways of knowing
a body. A gate had slammed shut

in the ice, setting its glass vaults
chittering. The blood froze in her

as she floated down, her sleeves
sailed her through ages of floe,

her pallid finger-ends radiated
splinters of light. Particles of silt

gathered like gold-dust round her
shrammed head. Her heart stilled.

Deep under the ice cap no-one
can see you, no-one can hear you

as you wolf the cold, as you knife
thin air with your cries –

*she was shrouded in silk, her skin
was blue with tattoos, her headdress*

*was as tall as a child. She was two
thousand years old;* she was two.

We did what we had to to save her,
sawed her open from throat to navel,

drilled a hole in her skull, trammelled
her in silver-foil; then breathed for her

with machines till a ghost stole across
the pane like frost-fur, the smoke of ice.

Particulare Care

...pray Let particulare care be taken off this child, As it will be call'd for Again;
— note left at the Foundling Hospital

When I dream about the children, my boy my girl,
  I dream them small-boned and wordless, as if again
I've turned my back, forgotten to come home

to feed them and need to find my way back to grace
  beyond forgiving. Their dream-selves are always just-born
with their adult faces on, full of a sweet anxious daylight

I can barely look at, standing here on the edge
  of deep water. I do not deserve them, these foundlings,
whom I will call out for again and again in the orphanage of night.

The Good Daughters

after Paula Rego

How to strike a bargain
with the teeth only slightly
bared –

How to lip-read the lubricities
that flit across the eyes
of men in the street –

How to wear a strong face
like those of the raven-haired old ladies
riding the Lisbon metro –

How to delay the menses
with herbs
and a foul-mouthed prayer –

How to take the camera
and its black shroud
by surprise –

How to bring on the menses
with other herbs,
the ones like crochet-hooks –

How to wield the body
like an archangel
encased in a crinoline –

How to arrange a husband
across the lap
as if he were a baby –

How to receive
the kindness
of other women.

The Village

after Paula Rego

How the pencil squawks on the paper,
how the chickens croak inside her pockets
like the noise people make when their nails

are being pulled and the cat's got their tongues
– she heard it from her grandma, who sat
with her crabbed hands over the girl's face

and all the while, full of kindness and rage,
she was breastfeeding a baby with the head
of a man. It's enough to make your flesh crawl,

wake up, wake up, you can't bear to sleep
on your own, you might dream the child's
stopped breathing or is floating in the sea,

drowned and still so hungry. The man-baby
has been crouched on the floor for days
weeping into his nappy; very soon he'll become

president and put a stop to all these tortures.
Grandma has climbed into bed wearing her hat;
it's cold, and the children are nowhere to be seen.

Personajes

after Remedios Varo

1. Orinoco

'Exploración de las fuentes del río Orinoco', oil on canvas, 1959

Where does the self come from, with its soft hoods
and closed buttonholes?
Of what slubs and gabardines is it made?
Whose are its afternoons, those up-rivers paddled
by anxiety and boredom in the same measure,
whose little winged ship
in a forest of cut-out wishes?

Some of my selves, sombre and intrepid,
feel neither hunger nor thirst;
I do not know their names. They have gone on
without me.

Some of them are embroidered bowls
meekly appearing on every ledge of my palace
like cupped hands.
What can they catch but the serene news
of someone else's rescue,
seeps of light floating downstream
to where I fret with shame and envy?

Others wear their Schiaparelli next to the skin
– shoe-hat or lobster-dress, crocodillo,
veils and tears.
They canter on high-heeled pilgrimages
through the island's flooded woods
tuning in to documentaries on their boat-shaped radios.
It seems unlikely the source will find them.

The poles melt. The gazetteer is in the pocket I cannot reach.

2. Ascension

'Ascensión al monte análogo', oil on triplay, 1960

I wake on a small plank of early morning,
the night hours of unsupported self-study
abandoned for the wistful disciplines
of list-making, of listening to messages hidden
in my telephone – I'm infatuated with gadgetry,
how the newly-sprung breeze fans my pinafore,
how my wristwatch escapes into a ship's quadrant.

The volcano behind me is full of digital spaces
like the empty-hearted bungalows
of an advanced society; its brook-waters
are everything to me. All day I surf the borders
of unrequited memory, navigating by fingertip.
This is not the end of the world, even if I buried
a box of lockets in the ash with their faces on.

If you would climb higher,
pay no account to public opinion. Don't
pick the flowers.
These two truths: it is already too late.
Be kind.

3. Laboratory

'Creación de las aves', oil on Masonite, 1957

Formula: I have my owl-mask on and the windows
that cannot be closed, I have made a miniature Stradivarius
to use as stethoscope; I have stoked the sensorium.

Modus operandi: a stylus, held in the painting hand,
is connected by the violin to the heart, you may feel
a quiet vibration in your chest-bones. The other hand

holds a magnifier. In separate pipettes, blood, egg, sky,
the primary birdsongs (this is not rocket science),
hatch their cantatas. I put on feather leggings,

sprinkle food. Outcome: a still-life of goldcrests
galvanised by rays of Pythagorean light, ensouled.
Try to attain a state of not-thinking; continue playing.

4. Minotaur

'El minotauro', oil on Masonite, 1959

Canto hondo. Bedtime stories.
There was a bull, his flanks white
as apple blossom, eyes blacker
than blood. Bull-I was down

on my snowy knees eating grass,
whisking flies. I was medicine.
Now all that's left of the lily ponds
and frescoed palace are its lino-tiles

and blank walls, the dust of koi-bones
in unswept corners. Or is it history
you want, a keyhole into the future?
At any moment the crescent moons

on my head will mutate into organs
of light, a hydraulics of heifer-milk
and Indian pearls; the squirm
in my right hand is an iron key

in a tight space, this unblinking gaze
is my poker face worn with a smile.
Covering your king with my queen
I sigh: Today of all days, the day

I began to smell like a woman,
the day I started washing the red
out of my clothes, I knew this was
my labyrinth, all its echoes

and strangers. As I tap-dance
on the tips of my mary-jane hooves,
you can see the placebo effect
is real, my costume period-perfect.

5. Personage

'Personaje', oil on Masonite, 1958

Nothing is what it seems, it takes
the entire span of the human voice
to improvise a space in the ruins
where the sense of weightlessness
can materialise, a pile of clothing
appear at the foot of a tree
like an undreamt dream. The room

grows yellower with dusk, its woods
point to underground water sources,
the still-sleeping *primum frigidum*,
or sometimes one of those silent dolls
a child describes her world with
behind closed doors. I was tearing up
bits of paper in the hope of finding

a way back, all I wanted was to live
without trash and the casual
discourtesies of the rich. The music
was distant, lunar, but these are not
the merciful things I set out to say.
I was leaning too far out of the window,
turning to absolute zero as I fell.

Azulejo

In 1492 Abu Abdallah (known in Spanish as Boabdil), the last
Moorish king of Spain, surrendered the kingdom of Granada
with a cry of desolation, *'el último suspiro del Moro'*

In the small hot dark Mr Abu Abdallah
lies down on the glazed tiles
his robes folded in a neat pile beside him
his arms gravely holding the shape
of the woman who gravely holds him
as his eyes fill with the night
and he marvels at how there's a word
for every phenomenon in this life
azimuth meaning angle or bearings
algebra meaning reunion of broken parts
algorithm meaning the art of preparing jallab
alcove meaning domed vault
attar meaning perfume – and yet no word
for the way the stuccoed arches
are yawning over him and the scent
of burning catches the back of his throat
how the bones in his buttocks bruise
the thin *mattress* spread out for him
meaning something thrown to the ground
and his eyes can see nothing but night
not *azure* meaning sky-blue nor *zenith*
meaning the sun at its peak
and his mind wanders back to a lost land
the treasure they jettisoned in fleeing
average meaning the proportionate sharing
of storm-damaged goods the basket of *limes*
meaning lemons the chess-board
set out with its king uncastled *rukhkh*
meaning chariot or breath of the phoenix
the queen's black tears streaking her face
kohl meaning the night in her eyes
or the *zero* meaning cipher meaning nought
like the subtle body's sigh as it goes.

Magellan

Quem sabe se a bordo não seguiria um cistre para acompanhar,
nas noites de calmaria, toadas de marinheiros
— Cristina Drios, 'Mar Magalhães'

For a day and an evening
   we were gathered in an old palace

on the outskirts of the city whose language
   I could read but could not speak.

Beyond the windows the garden floated
   adrift in a squall of low cloud;

the state-room's walls had long since let go
   their decorative papers and delicate frescos,

those electric blues, sea-greens and coral reds
   submitting little by little

to unnumbered summers and winters,
   the bare plaster underneath crazing

finer and finer with every passing century
   of stern atlantic weathers

until it had been transfigured
   into a cartography, endlessly

intricate, of some *terra* forever *incognita*.
   Voices echoed in the vast hall,

cascading down the bow-wave
   of the imperial staircase:

I heard them only as cries
   of sea-birds or a flight of songs

inside the stone. Sometimes the tide
   sounds like a foreign tongue,

escutastes as histórias e as canções
   sob os céus estrelados de todos os oceanos[†]

– though tonight, becalmed in mid-voyage,
   Fernão de Magalhães peers out

over a body of water glassy and taciturn as rock.
   Daylight will be a slur of dazzle and haze,

his heart all *saudade*.
   In the palace a woman began playing for us,

candlelight caught the silver fan
   adorning the guitar's neck,

and what I heard was the lament of water
   being poured out on dry ground,

the salt-laden gravity of desire.
   Fernão, becalmed in his cabin, dreams

that when if ever he sets sail again
   he will reach not land and home but the edge

lying in wait at the far west of the mind,
   the sickening sooner-or-later tilt and lurch

on the brink of sleep
   for which there is no goodnight prayer

in his or ours or any language,
   that his maps and charts are ink on water,

that the future is an immensity
   of heave and drop, as intimate

and terrifying as the distance between
 us and the star-clouds that will ship his name.

The music does what music can:
 this hairline of gold

running through, then into, the dark.

*   Translation: Who knows if, on calm nights, a cittern did not follow them
    on board to accompany the sailors' ditties

†   Translation: you have listened to the stories and the songs /
    beneath the starry skies of all the oceans.

Say Goodbye, Catullus

after 'Say Goodbye, Catullus, to the Shores of Asia Minor',
Cy Twombly, 1972–1994, oil, acrylic, oil stick, crayon on three canvases

We moderns are made of lost cities: Athens, Troy, Rome,
their graffiti and generals, their masks and hallucinogens;
or else Verona, Tomis, Alexandria, whose bisexual poets

and citizens-of-nowhere we are, stirring immensities of disquiet;
we are the teeming *civitas*, labyrinthine and violent,
leaking epithalamia and civil war beneath the wheatfields –

and now it's spring again, big skies, his sun-warmed flesh
under your hand, the raw memory of it, and the land convulsing
in gouts of song, uprushes of longing. Time to move on,

you say, but sorrow too has been over-wintering
like some life-form hungry for heat and rut; and now
the jism of grief erupts in a bud-burst of jilt and mucus –

these little chthonic gods are your fellow-travellers,
Gaius Valerius, though you're barely tethered to the earth –
and suddenly your knees buckle with the ache of it,

a barbaric anguish that could blow your brains out –
pain is not an epistemic problem, it's a *cri de sang*,
blood in the yolk, and you – we – a lifetime away from home.

What Is Not Lost

Just sometimes, not everything is lost;
possibilities persist through burn-out

and roof-fall, the ash-heap of oak rafters
and puddles of grey water where panes

of ruby and sapphire, awe and magnificence swim
in the shadows. Transported to childhood,

exhilarated, exhausted, we greet ourselves
and each other as matter, clotted and weeping,

as marks half-buried in a scrawl of vast allusions,
trying our best (which is never enough)

to inhabit the space that has suddenly emptied.
Call it mystery, call it a lacework of stone,

call it a lost cause. Call it a rose.
We are its elements, the light is Kyrie, all-mercy,

call it blaze or the cloudburst that puts out the blaze,
this is not yet an answer to which the question

is hope, that brief blossom of flesh on bare bones
before the sky caves in, the hum of bees like a furnace.

Two Rivers Press has been publishing in and about Reading
since 1994. Founded by the artist Peter Hay (1951–2003),
the press continues to delight readers, local and further afield,
with its varied list of individually designed,
thought-provoking books.